Farm Animals

Los Animales de Granja

Moo

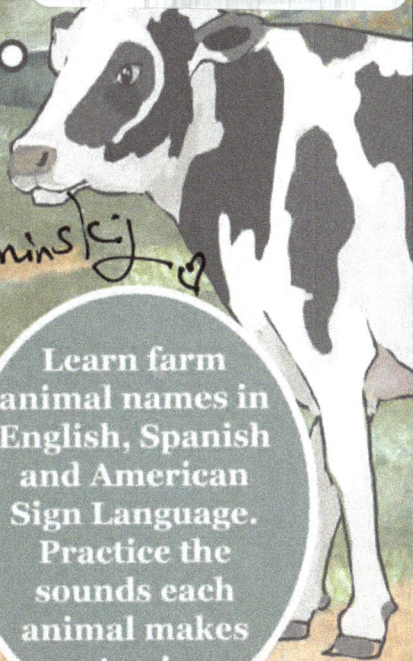

Learn farm animal names in English, Spanish and American Sign Language. Practice the sounds each animal makes too !

By Claire Suminski
Illustrated by Susan Swedlund and Julia Wolff

Reading is an Exciting Adventure

Learning is an exciting adventure!

Farm   de Granja
English   Spanish

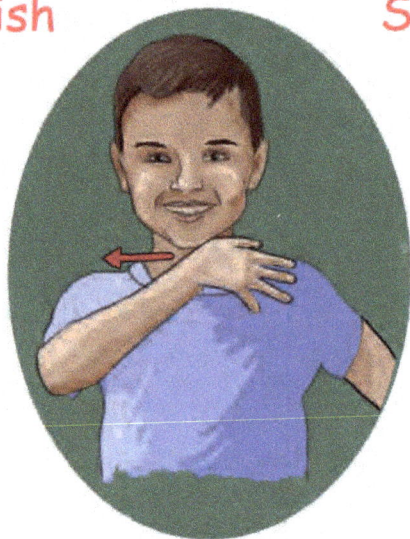

American Sign Language*

All the signs depicted in this book are from the
website https://www.lifeprint.com/
and are current as of August 2022.

Copyright 2022 by Claire Suminski
All rights reserved.

No part of this book may be used or reproduced in any
manner whatsoever without written permission.
Contact Suminski Family Books,
32 Jim Berry Road, Franklin, NC 28734

First Edition
ISBN 979-8-9856781-3-0
Library of Congress Control Number: 2022916237

A Note to Parents:

This book has been written to be of interest to a variety of ages. Your toddler will enjoy pointing at the farm pictures and hearing you make the sound each animal makes. As your child grows, point out the animal featured on each page and ask him or her to name the animal, then make the corresponding sound and finally practice spelling the easiest names. Early grades will enjoy making their own English/Spanish Farm animal flash cards. All ages (Including parents!) will want to try making the American Sign Language animal signs. This is a simple book, but in a variety of ways will be fun for the whole family.

Communication skills are so important. I hope this book will help build a desire in your children to communicate even a few words to someone else in his or her language. Our intent at Suminski Family Books is that all of our books will be useful in very practical ways and also spread joy.

Happy Reading,
Claire Suminski
and the SFB Staff

English   Spanish

cow / la vaca

American Sign Language sign for Cow

Keep your thumb on your forehead, then twist your wrist down so that your pinkie finger is pointing slightly downward.

It is like the horn of the cow is moving up and down.

Chicken / el pollo
Chick / el pollito

American Sign Language sign for Chicken and Chick

1. With your hand up by your mouth use your fore finger and your thumb to make a beak.

2. Bring your two finger together like the beak is closing. Do the closing motion twice quickly.

English   Spanish

rooster/ el gallo

American Sign Language sign for Rooster

Tap your forehead twice with the tip of your thumb, keeping the two closest fingers pointing up. This is like the comb on the rooster's head.

English   **Spanish**

sheep / la oveja

American Sign Language sign for Sheep

With your right hand make a "scissors" with your first two fingers. Have the "scissors" move up the arm, while at the sametime having your "scissors" open and close. It is as if you are shearing the sheep.

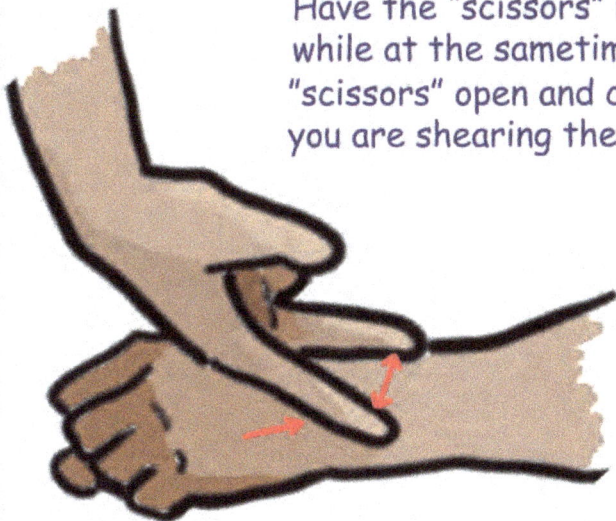

English   Spanish

pig / el cerdo

American Sign Language sign for Pig

With your fingers pointing to the left, (if you are right handed) bend and unbend your hand several times from the knuckles. Your wrist should not move. The fingers do not "wiggle." They bend and unbend from the large knuckles.

English   **Spanish**

goat/ la cabra

American Sign Language sign for Goat

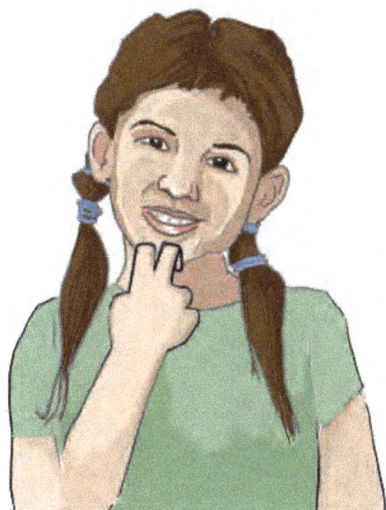

1. The handshape starts and stays in a "bent-V" shape. Start at the chin.

2. Move your hand quickly upward.

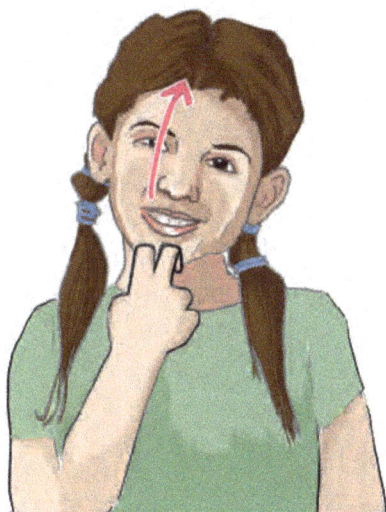

3. Bring your hand, keeping it in the "bent-V" shape, to the top of your forehead.

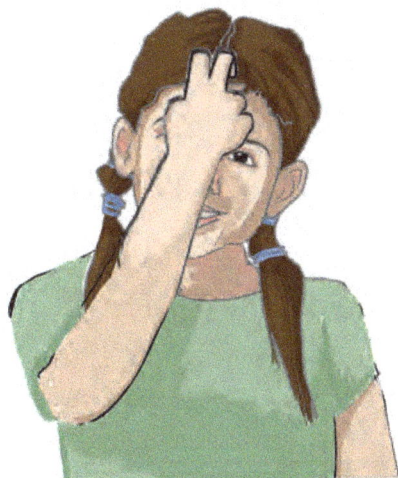

It is like you are showing the beard of the goat and then it's horns.

neigh

English   Spanish

horse / el caballo

American Sign Language sign for Horse

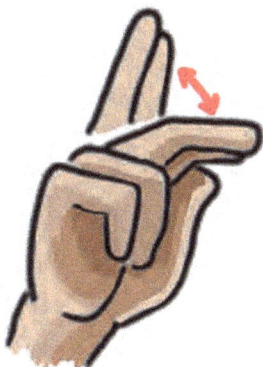

Place your thumb on your right temple, or a little higher, point your two fingers closest to your thumb up. Bend and unbend your first two fingers a couple times, like the twitching of the horse's ear.

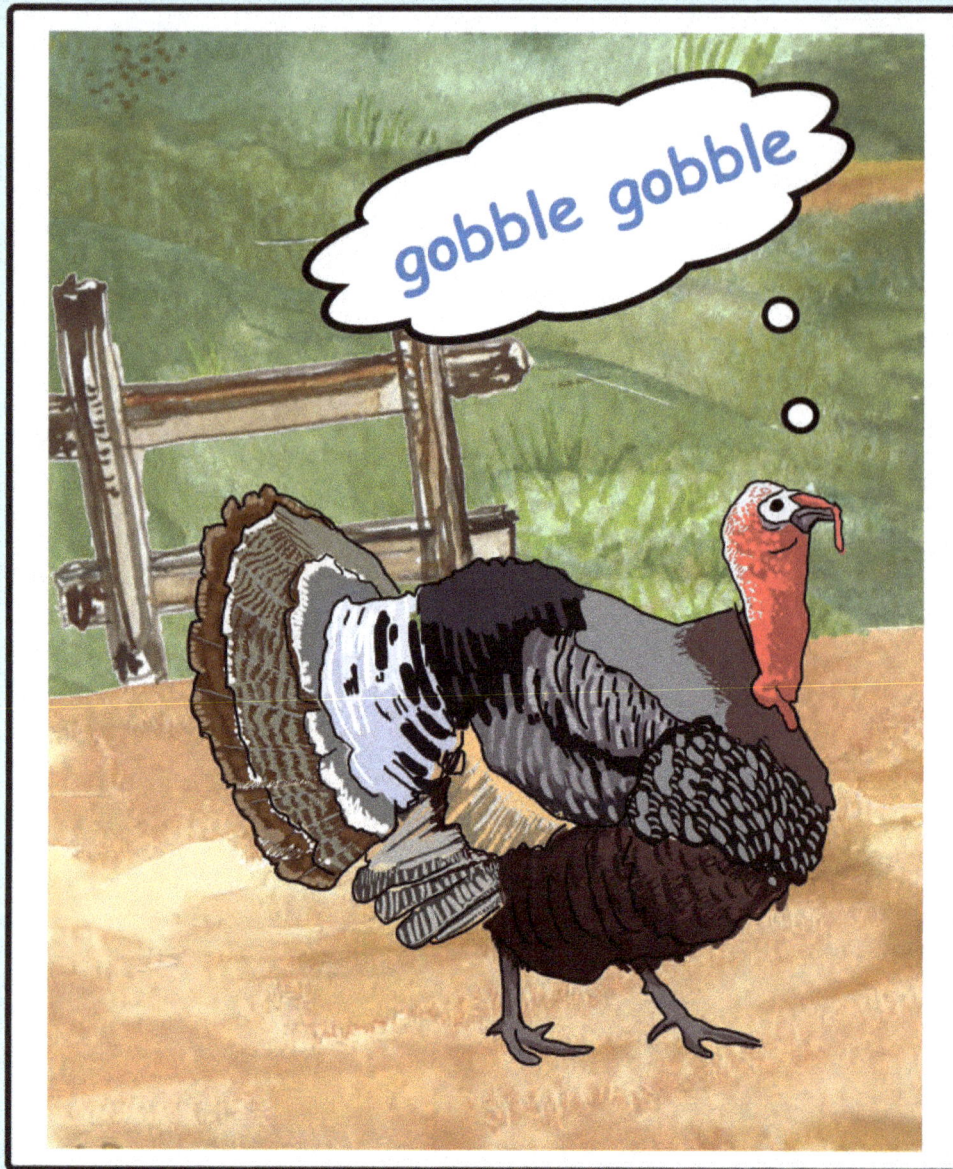

English   Spanish

turkey / el pavo

American Sign Language sign for Turkey

Hang your forefinger and your thumb under your chin and wiggle your two hanging fingers around.

Wiggle it a couple times as if it were a "wattle." (A wattle is the flap of skin connecting the turkey's throat and head.)

English	Spanish
dog /	el perro, la perra
	(male) (female)
puppy /	el perrito, la perrita
	(male) (female)

American Sign Language sign for Dog and Puppy

To sign dog or puppy simply snap your fingers 2 times in a row.

English   Spanish

donkey / el burro

American Sign Language sign for Donkey

The sign for "donkey" shows the bending ear of a donkey. Do the movement twice.

It can be produced with one hand or two.

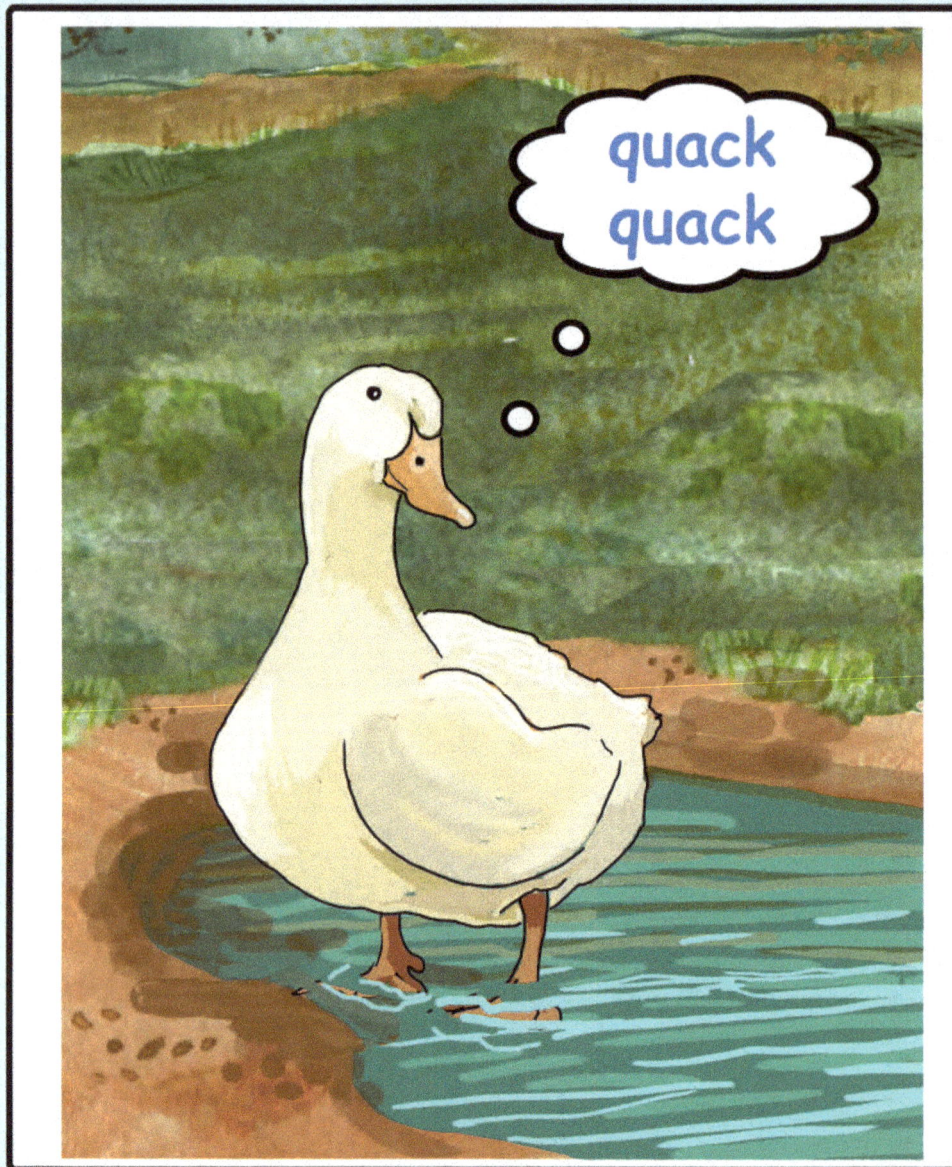

English   **Spanish**

duck / el pato

American Sign Language sign for Duck

The sign for "duck" opens and closes a "bill" twice as if you were quacking twice.
Make this hand shape by extending the index finger, middle finger, and thumb.

English	Spanish
cat /	el gato, la gata
	(male) (female)
kitten/	el gatito, la gatita
	(male) (female)

American Sign Language sign for Cat and Kitten

1. Start with your hand under your nose by your mouth.

2. Move your hand outward and slightly down.

3. Bring your forefinger and thumb together as you move outward.

Make these motions like you are stroking the whiskers of a cat.

English   Spanish

bees / las abejas

American Sign Language sign for Bees

1.

2.

3.

Show the concept of being stung on the cheek (1) then swatting the bee away (2,3).

Enjoy all of our books for young readers
in our Reading is an Exciting Adventure Series!

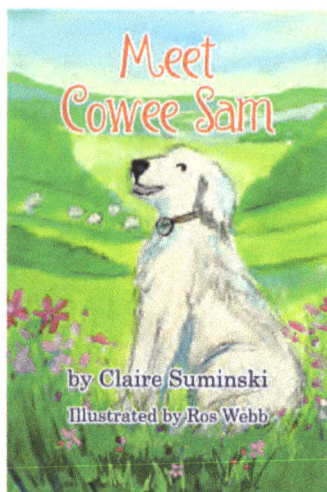

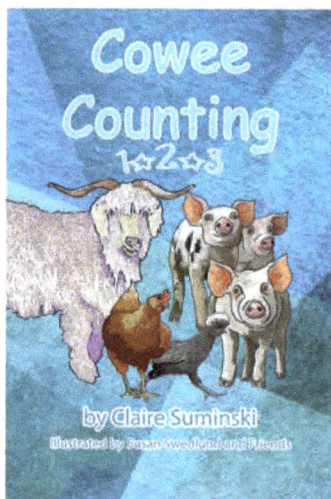

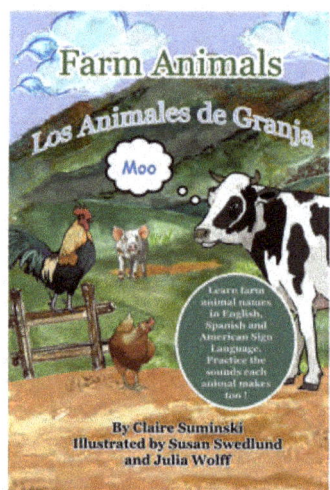

Meet
Cowee Sam
by Claire Suminski
Illustrated by Ros Webb

Wee-Tee
The Farm Cat and Her "EE" Adventures
By
Claire Suminski

Cowee
Counting
1•2•3
by Claire Suminski
Illustrated by Susan Swedlund and Friends

Farm Animals
Los Animales de Granja
Moo
Learn farm animal names in English, Spanish and American Sign Language. Practice the sounds each animal makes too !
By Claire Suminski
Illustrated by Susan Swedlund and Julia Wolff

Order these as well as all of
our other books at:
www.suminskifamilybooks.com
Free games and activities too!

www.ingramcontent.com/pod-product-compliance
Lightning Source LLC
Chambersburg PA
CBHW052125030426
42335CB00025B/3128